Just This

Just This

Poems by

Judith Janoo

© 2023 Judith Janoo. All rights reserved.
This material may not be reproduced in any form, published,
reprinted, recorded, performed, broadcast,
rewritten, or redistributed without
the explicit permission of Judith Janoo.
All such actions are strictly prohibited by law.

Cover art by Helen Stork
Author photo by Steven Cahill
Cover design by Shay Culligan

ISBN: 978-1-63980-368-2

Kelsay Books
502 South 1040 East, A-119
American Fork, Utah 84003
Kelsaybooks.com

Acknowledgements

Grateful acknowledgment is made to the editors of the journals and anthologies who first published the following poems. The poems, sometimes in earlier versions, appeared as follows:

After Effects: "Salt Air Heritage," "Chiang Mai, City of Temples," "The Edge of the Gorge"
The Bangalore Review: "Johor Bahru"
Fish Anthology: "Sugar Kelp"
The Main Street Rag: "He Dreamed of Flying," "What Lasts"
The Mountain Troubadour: "Machias Seal Island," "Bear Cub," "Sweet Elegy," "Perfection," "Phoebe," "Route 132," "Marking Time"
Paper Dragon, Drexel University: "What I Want to Hold Onto"
Pedestal Magazine: "The Edge of the Gorge"
The Pierian: "Fall Song," "Invitation," "What Circled Us"
The Poem City Anthology: "Well Being"
The Poets Touchstone: "Seed Exchange," "Yoga of Poetry," "Winter Island," "Lament," "Hanging Flannel," "This Dance," "Just This"
Sow's Ear Poetry Review: "Men at the General Store"
The Well Being Economy Alliance: "Well Being"

Awards

Anita McAndrews Prize for Human Rights Poetry: "Well Being"
Arthur Wallace Peach Memorial Award: "Making Time"
The Carol Lee Vail Prize for Emerging Poets: "Machias Seal Island"
Chris White Memorial Award (runner-up): "Time"
Fish Poetry Prize (finalist): "Sugar Kelp"
The Goldstein Memorial Award: "Bear Cub"
Mary Margaret Audette Memorial Award (runner-up): "Yoga of Poetry"
Music and Word Collaborative Presentation: "The Wind," "Salt Air Heritage," "Edge of the Gorge"
Reader's Choice, Poetry Society of Vermont: "What Keeps Us"

Dedications

I'm indebted to Louise Rader for her insightful, poetic sensibilities, and to April Ossmann who helped shape this manuscript with her generous and skillful mentoring.

I'm indebted to the members of the Barton Wednesday Poets' Group for constant inspiration and mutual support, to the Vermont Studio Center for invaluable space and encouragement to write when I first needed it, to The Frost Place, and to the Poetry Society of Vermont.

I'm indebted to workshop leaders: Baron Wormser, Aimee Nezhukumatathil, Campbell McGrath, Max Ekstrom, Martha Rhodes and Maudelle Driskell, the Burlington Writer's Workshop, and Jimmy Pappas for his weekly poetry-immersion events.

Thanks to Helen Stork for the cover artwork, and to Kelsay Books, Delisa and Karen, for making the publication process smooth, thoughtful and professional.

Special thanks to the late, Mame Willey, for believing in me as a poet from the get-go.

Love and gratitude to Vincent for sharing the Malaysian culture for 27 years; to our children, Angela, Tony, and Mandy; to my dear hearts, Connor, Logan, and Claire; and to S.J. Cahill, for gifting humor and companionship.

"Fall Song," "Invitation," and "What We Had to Learn" are for Vincent

"Marking Time" is for Connor

"Just This" is for Logan

"What Lasts" and "He Dreamed of Flying" are for my *Māmaṉār,* father-in-law

Contents

I.

Route 132	17
Bear Cub	19
Machias Seal Island	21
Salt Air Heritage	22
The Zipper	24
The Clammer	27
What We Had to Learn	28
Phoebe	29
Can't Steal a Beat from Our Swing	30
What I Want to Hold Onto	31
How to Beaver	33
This Dance	35
Hanging Flannel	37
Johor Bahru	39

II.

What Keeps Us	43
The Edge of the Gorge	44
Drawn	45
Sugar Kelp	46
The Wind	48
Quilts of Gees Bend	50
Like a Leaf	52
Men at the General Store	54
Winter Island	55
He Dreamed of Flying	56
Perfection	57
Time	58
Fall Song	59
Sweet Elegy	60

Invitation	62
Chiang Mai, City of Temples	64
After the Long Winter	65
As If One	66

III.

Well Being	69
Aubade	70
Yoga of Poetry	71
Marking Time	72
Lament	73
Last Night the Supermoon	74
Seed Exchange	76
What Circled Us	78
The Way You Pick	79
Just This	81
What Lasts	82
Voice of the Tide	84
Letter to My Grandson Through the Wardrobe	86
Why I Called in Thinking of Rumi	88

"They will soar on wings like eagles, they will run and not grow weary, they will walk and not be faint."
—Isaiah 40:31

I.

Route 132

Alright,
I'll pull over
and let you pass

on this
fog-hung
winding road.

I'm not
hurrying, not
tonight.

I'll give way
gladly, as I look
for a shoulder

to hold me,
where turns
are sharper

than wit,
and seeing
means feeling

a way forward.
Did I just miss
a clearing

braking out
of your high beams'
blinding?

Each town meeting
we let go
of straightening

this road, meandering
with the river,
settling for stasis,

for danger,
only in haste—
your rush

once was mine,
the impatience
to get wherever

there was—
and then
what?

Bear Cub

Eyes closed at first,
wintering inside the earth,
black matted fur

dampness pressing soft eyelids
shut to outlast frost
heaving around him,

he belly crawls, paws
a way out, his store of chest,
ribs and shoulder flesh lost;

the long dormant yearling
recalls insects, beeswax,
purple berries pouring

into grasping claws, juice
drooling his chin, less greed
than strength and instinct.

Orphaned by a poor
beechnut fall, left
with the unfed restiveness

of his lumbering;
he'll hunt the old trail,
the new, with purblind eyes,

dig through waste,
the lingering scent
of bacon grease, fish

entrails, knocking loose
his dim view—
weakened, disoriented

after so much darkness,
he—and we—long
to see the sun.

But it takes time
to open our eyes
once we've shut them.

Machias Seal Island

In the quiet of shared borderland,
in the solitary air, fog lifting off

the Maine coast and Canada's Bay,
in the lighthouse, the keeper

keeps sculpting darkness
in the silence that is the island,

the borderland's weathered rock
and scrubgrass, old Passamaquoddy

fishing grounds so remote,
neither country claimed ownership,

sharing the sculptor of darkness,
wind-riven grasses and eroding rock,

the flagman for fishing boats
the petrels, razorbills, and prim puffins

emerging from rock crevices, awkward,
stocky, but dressed to a T, safety-orange

bills stuffed with supper: herring,
briny strands of bladderwrack,

waving surrender where no treaties
sculpt the joined silence, no claim

widens abstract differences, where sea
and shore peacefully share a border,

and the keeper shines a light
on conduct in deep water.

Salt Air Heritage

I am from the rocks and shore
of fishermen, lobster boats,

dove gray mornings that rise
from blackness over water.

I am from shell shock,
impermeable days

Dad reached for safety
after Omaha Beach.

I am from homemade
biscuit kitchens, Mom

heating salty chowders,
from clam flats, mackerel traps,

gulls cruising for cast-offs,
from moonlight sieved by cedars

scraping bedroom windows,
awake to long angry silences,

the suffering of a gentle man,
made infantryman,

and a pearl, her shell worn down
to sand. I am from

a scenic shore, a border
where I hid to escape

the eight-room cape,
stone-walled acres of hayfields

above a harbor of broken glass,
fear and laughter ground smooth

by constant movement,
wave subsuming wave,

each indistinguishable
from the next.

The Zipper

*an amusement ride with strong vertical G-forces, spins
and a noted sense of unpredictability*

O, summer wattage
baby-oiled skin sizzling,
    erupting,
transistor radios playing *Louie Louie,*
mumbled phrases passing over
       inexperienced boys, good girls
in floral bikinis, saving themselves,

slow dancing *Stairway to Heaven,*
as Armstrong lands in moon boots,
   and waves move satin sheets
over rocks and gray sand.

Root beer bottles with two straws,
an older boy looking on
   from the hood of his Torino,
heating the salt spray
with his gaze,
     melting the peonies
from our bikinis, an attention
half-craved, half-disdained
   by the innocent,
      the exposed.

That summer leaked Pentagon papers
Marvin Gaye's, *Mercy Mercy Me,*
   we believed, watusied, twisted,
protested, aimed our future

away from a war-torn past
     not knowing how far
we'd be asked to go.

O, summer wattage,
steam off his MG,
    far out, make out
to *Fire and Rain,* go steady,
but don't go all the way.

Frightened, flattered,
dating a collegiate.
    Go to the fair with me?

Shoulders slick rock,
blur of skin, air
    sparked with heat,
each cage flip, resist
the tumbling within
        another tumbling,
its unforeseen upending.

His MG humming.
Let's find someplace quiet.
    Thighs, fingers,
stake my reputation
on love first, forever,
        hold back.

Hey Jude. Aren't you horny?
Hands in my lap longing,
    but I was green. What did he mean?
Should I save face, and say:
we invaded Cambodia,
      talk about Kent State,
try to save our planned
next date, not express

what he guessed
before he stood me up,
    left me a window of hunger
not knowing how far
he'd asked me to go.

The Clammer

In the clam beds, in the sheltering cove,
in the slow draining of waves
his skiff grounded by low tide,
alone and bent, he works the flats.

In the slow draining of waves,
he feels for steamers,
alone and bent, he works the flats,
breathing sea lavender and salt's tang.

He feels for steamers
as he feels for her at night,
breathing sea lavender and her salt tang
as she kneads his tide-bound back, unfolding him.

Feeling for her at night
is like the ocean about to turn,
as she kneads his tide-bound back, unfolding him
in her rhythm, that gives his life meaning,

like the ocean about to turn,
with his skiff grounded by low tide
he opens to the rhythm, his life's meaning
in the clam beds, in the sheltering cove.

What We Had to Learn

Cod fritters sizzle in the saucepan as you pour
smooth cognac into jelly jars, our first dinner

alone, you flying back soon after we met
when my mother praised your humor, your ease,

the way you ate three lobsters and asked for more.
I taste lemon butter on your lips, offer you crab dip

you receive as if knowing you'd find me
in this Down East town of scallop boats,

abandoned sardine factories, and breakwatered
whirlpools, undeterred at all we had to learn.

You pour more cognac to top off my glass,
gaze as if already you see me frying mutton curry

the winter our two ewes would lamb, and the ram butt
me against the barn manger, as if you'd already fainted

seeing our first daughter born, held your breath to help
slow our son's delivery in the crowded ward, or nestled

my aching sacrum in our own bed, awaiting our youngest,
rubbing my back, as you slide a tittle of cod across your

upper lip and coax me to taste it. As you would teach me
to eat meat with my hands, suction marrow from bone,

invite lone travelers in for a warm meal so far from home,
to see you slicing onions and radishes so fine they swam

in the vinegar, like minnows just visible beneath the surface.

Phoebe

You taught me to circle words
in coverless books you kept
in a corner by the couch:

yours, then *mine,* then *ours,*
as I learned to read new words,
searching already-circled pages.

I still see you in the kitchen chair
you and Dad bought at the prison store.
It held you as you fostered children,

taught *hope, care, safe,* how to hold
graphite, form alphabet loops. My foster
sister learned *good, smart, worthy,*

adding weight to her boney frame,
and I became protector, *helpful,
dutiful, generous,* until *selfish*

appeared with *dreams, ideas,*
yet still responsible, afraid
of the day something would happen to you.

You would fall from your chair,
and not rise again, and I
would need to find words

for my sister to circle,
first with my hands,
then with my heart.

Can't Steal a Beat from Our Swing

The kind of beat that brings your baby back,
   that triple step, rock step—open-out savoy
style. Not a tempo that takes its long slow time,

it's a jive beat, eight count, three-quartering drumskin.
   I remember our first lindy low, knees bent
into our soles, into the floor, into the downbeat,

the strong beat, what we needed to take the weight.
   Did I mention the whip, the spin, the basket—
his hand chasing my back, my hand pressed

to his fresh-aired flannel, shouldering the pulse,
   the horn's hollow brass doubling back
for a cry. The upbeat, the cross-arm, the dip,

the room moves at the edge of the pause
   when it all smooths. The kind of tempo
no one messes with, no grabbing your man for war,

not in the turn, the aerial, the wrap of this dance.
   No stolen boyhood, no shock to the bone,
not one note missed when we step onto the floor.

What I Want to Hold Onto

My hand's lifelines palm-width,
picking up the phone
to tell a friend I'm sorry
I'm not a phone person. I'll call,
but not often. I've tried.

A pencil, strips of notepaper,
return envelopes I won't return,
lists of those I need
to ring up, working up
to the phone's heavy weight,
checking off one name
each day.

In my hands the weight
of not living up
to the outgoing need
of me.

In my hands polished glass,
green, icy-blue,
the ocean smoothed
of edges jagged as mine.

In my hands, sea water,
dripping between my fingers
when I reach for more
of what I have not worked for,

wading into pools,
in deepening water
miles from a phone,
from the call
about my mother,

knowing she'd never again
comb the wet sand,
carry driftwood home
to put on the shelf
above the only phone we owned.

How to Beaver

If we could live on a river,
build a dome for a home,
cooled by lazy currents

we slowed to shallow pools,
if we could see underwater
at night with our lifelong mate,

our kit apprentices filtering streams,
packing mud into hemlock crisscrosses,
warding off predators

with our handy castoreum.
If we could fell aspens, birch,
with iron incisors,

would we despair
if our sculpted universe
were torn apart,

un-bridging riversides.
Would we stomp our wronged feet
slap back with hateful tales,

or would we repair
our lodge's brittle beauty,
make a moat for dragonflies,

blue strands of heron,
feed lily roots
rising like natal cords

to the grassy surface?
Would we make spillways
and passageways tilt upstream?

Tell me whether we'd restrain a river
if our lives depended on it.

This Dance

My *māmiyār* pounds garlic and ginger
   in the stone mortar she wore down
      early in her marriage. New to cold
New England from Johor Bahru,
   she adds chili and coriander, hands me
      the cutting board. *Here, the onions.*

Their sharp post-partum moodiness
   half screens the acrid smell
      of *sambal blanchan,* fried shrimp paste
I will never learn to love.
   Her English weak, my Tamil anemic,
      the wok crackles with star anise,
scent penetrating as light through her orange silk,
   wrapped and draped, pleated at her waist.

Finished? She snatches the knife. *Like this.*
   Onion fine as a spray of baby's breath.
      Easy to make chicken curry.

Sleep-deprived, milk expressing, baby
   wailing, innate lust for mustard seed,
      cardamom pods, my reprieve—
to close the door, nurse our newborn,
   taste of sweetened milk until
      the orange flare pulls the baby from me.
Now the other side. See. It is better.

She must think this new mother knows no more
   than the balsams, sprouting quickly,
      eclipsed and withered by hardwoods.
My son breastfed this high. She presses
   sunset mid-thigh, silk rustling
      as she leaves, leaving the door open.

If only I could reach my mother,
   at rest where I can't follow,
     ask her how to stand
three months of foreign instruction,
   and find common mother's ground
     so I can come to love

my husband's culture, learn
   to fold silk pleats at my waist,
     make stay in place
as we move to a new rhythm.

Hanging Flannel

Grief appears, a lily spear
in winter's listless grasses,
robins pecking last year's

radish bed. Hear them
flapping the clotheslines—
sound of wings—bluebird's

wasp hunt, phoebe's beetled
hovering, mother's nesting sighs
rising against gravity.

Grief comes glimpsed
in a stranger's surprise
of kindness, making me ache

for the screen door's slap,
her on the granite back step,
hanging frayed towels

and loose housedresses,
waving to the wind
lozenging morning's throat,

salt air dampening her skirt
and slack, knee-length socks,
his flannel shirts

with war sweat set in. Grief
creaks, like the screen door hinge
opening on wafting cod chowder,

and the rusted pulley she tugs
as she steps into the lines
of dawn's constellation, just

beyond my reach.

Johor Bahru

The music of Johor Bahru
   is sitar strings
      plying breezes
off the South China Sea,
   fanning jasmine and lemongrass
      across verandas.

The music of Johor Bahru
   is rice pots popping,
      a kompang rhythm,
cashews softening in coconut and ghee,
   nasi biryani, beef satay,
      pandan leaves, sizzling like bees.

The music of Johor Bahru
   is rafflesia's red blare,
      whining *Aiyahs*. Hornbills
humming, monitor lizards
   clicking at chickens
      in the street.

The music of Johor Bahru
   is murmured *Assalam Allaikum,*
      it is *Shanti,* it is peace.
It is macaques in mangosteen
   trees chucking fruit,
      hee, hee, hee.

It's the music of Malays
   tapping rubber trees,
      Chinese miners, British
colonizers beating tin into profit,
   before the Japanese invasion
      captured your father.

The music of Johor Bahru
    is moon orchids, tiger orchids
        grafted to coral trees.
It is sea eagles' barking,
    prawn paste bubbling,
        your cumin-scented skin.

The music of Johor Bahru
    is succulent jungle drumming
        our cradle song,
your sarong swinging
    our babies
        between your knees.

II.

What Keeps Us

That Thanksgiving the Shendos,
our Pueblo friends, made atole
bread and we roasted turkey,
mashed potato and turnip
with garlic and cream,
spread our meal
on the big Formica table
sustained by skinny metal legs.
We heaped plates, and I said grace,
as the weight of our preparations bore down—
a harbinger metal *creak,*
a *scree,* then *whish*
of cascading plates
as the weakest leg
gave way.

Stunned, you salvaged the bird
and I the baby from the high chair,
as peas and cranberries swam
in the pool of squash and atole.
We might have wept had our friends
not seen whole nations fall.
They and their children
were glad to have passed-off
furnishings, and their heirloom
crystal laughter made us grateful,
so we re-arranged the remains
of our banquet to picnic
on the table-clothed floor.

The next day, we'd buy
heavy oak, a solid claw-foot
pedestal holding a knight's table,
the shape predating Columbus,
that keeps us from falling off
the face of the Earth.

The Edge of the Gorge

> *Man is by nature a political animal*
> —Aristotle

Canyons between us we can't understand.
Tell me, stranger, at this political divide,
what thresholds you failed to cross,

what you lost, that there's more
than nothing between us.

Freedom of thought, soft as lambs-ear,
cashmere, fragrant as thyme-walked
ground. Somewhere between love and hate,

atheist and saint. Even Tolstoy wrote first of war.
Peace falls like spring rain, an eagle feather.

Tell me, neighbor, of thresholds you failed
to cross, what you lost, that there's more
than nothing between us.

Can you divide this apple into three halves?
your daughter asked, feeding other hungry mouths

as she opened hers. Division as portioning.
Peace drops like a whisper between prairie warbler
and lark bunting, one feeder, tern and gull, one shore,

low tide and high. Over mountains, plains, drop
all your thoughts, friend, until edges give way, tell me
of thresholds you failed to cross, what you lost,

that there's more than nothing between us. I'm wary,
watching the broad-winged hawk circle, dive and rise.

Let stones shake from the ground up.
I want to feel the lift of your breath
on my cheek as you speak.

Drawn

Drawn to fishing boats,
diamonds of twine he mended,
set, checked at dawn,
hauling for a living,
and sharing with anyone
needing a meal if
he caught anything at all.

Drawn to smoked herring
strung along the cellarway,
cod jerky, canned sardines,
chowders simmering
in a red kitchen.

Drawn to September's plenty,
to its hail marking
the surviving harvest,
drawn to be the channel
to his Normandy landing—

*People sure were glad to see us,
some broke down.
Don't believe anybody
would want war*

*if they spent a minute
in a bombing raid.*

I'm drawn to the deep,
to melancholy,
innocence drained
from Edenic leaves—
to those who've dug foxholes
to shelter in, then find
they've moved on.
I'm drawn to the September in men.

Sugar Kelp

Do not go gentle into that good night
—Dylan Thomas

Sea garden of green lettuces, red mosses,
brown ribbons of sugar kelp caterpillared
just below the surface, spooling spores

around rope, above tiers of mussels, oysters—
the new farm, where hunger wraps as it grows,
eats poisons of land and air, while an old man's

bent head gives years to a bed, his hopes
to the cove, the return of the herring
folding into flakes of skin, white powder

of Gold Bond a daughter applies for him,
keeping him at home, and the caregivers with
bird names, Phoebe and Robyn, who come

mornings to wash him as sugar kelp is washed
by the waves, as it washes what the sea has taken
into itself. *All Rise,* say those who escaped

the firing on the beaches of his war laid down
inside him, near-cleansed, near-resigned as new
fishing ground, where no hook, no catch,

only soothing of a daughter's hands, until
she moves his lighter away from the oxygen tank,
and his pipe, his habit of reaching to ignite it.

He's slid down to the foot of the bed, one leg dangling
the rail, blankets bunched beneath him. He's wet.
"Can you push a little with your feet?" his daughter says.

"They don't work anymore."
She reminds him fishermen now farm the waters
he's spent a lifetime minding. "Growing sugar kelp."

"Seaweed," he says. "Algae. That stuff?"
Letting go of the buoys, his dories, the ocean and its scales.

The Wind

of the uncaught ball in the outfield,
southward threading vee
of hungry, *yahonking* geese,

the balloon man
the used car salesman
the real newsman.

Air seeping through a keyhole
old floor boards, a screen door.
The wind across wires

fences, continents,
migrating seeds to bog lands, rice fields,
prairie sweeps, trash heaps—

the air of rejection
the breath of silence.
I am the wind

of your night job, your day
job, the commute, dropping
dimes, falling behind.

The wind of climate change,
heat waves and hurricanes,
broken treaties of the displaced,

the lost, the wind across
fallen ancestors' gravestones,
a father passing over Shanghai

when his daughter couldn't
get back in time after
months by his bedside.

Wind of mercy, spring wind
vanishing winter, herding
the last faded leaves

into waiting woods,
choir wind of sacred singing,
lone heron winging over the cove,

hoot of red-throated loon.
I am the wind of remembering
and long goodbyes.

Quilts of Gees Bend

We travel far to see,
and cannot touch
what was patched

south of Selma
on a horseshoe bend
of the Alabama River,

plantation sewn in
denim, gingham,
fabric hymns,

unruled designs
shaped by candlelight.
What still had wear

reborn into a covering,
like a home, unfolding
in sections, of necessity

made from overalls
and faded yellow shifts
worn to thread in fields.

Would living here
with my dark husband
and mocha-skinned children,

cast us as remnants
of history, or would the world
see our ingenuity,

see what these women
pieced in hard-worn colors,
bordered with tones

of unfolding heroes,
Mandela, Annan, and Maathai,
as they pried cotton from the boll,

added a pant leg growing
from an uneven sleeve
washed of blood.

Like a Leaf

Blushing green,
brushing my palm,
       falling
   aloft
as the slightest breath
of wind catches its stem,

as if taking its hand,
lifting it from me
as it was lifted
       from where it formed,
   budded
tendering a tree's teeth,
sweetest taste of anticipation.

Love, like a leaf,
displays no vanity
as I trace its yellow veins;
       it waves
   as if it wants to play,
to let me feel how paper thin
its membranes, spotted from sun,
from living out its season,

but not losing itself, even as I preserve it
between sheets of waxed paper,
       muting its sheen
   to hold its crimson face
in future days to the light.

What I'd have missed
had this leaf been left
to fade
       not made a red splash
  over pages I leaf through
to choose words
for love,

like a leaf
made gossamer by time,
dropping into my palm
       while others drift,
   huddle, pile against the wind
as I wait
to jump in.

Men at the General Store

from a photograph of the Barton County Fair

When the fair comes to town, men in their Sunday best
line the general store steps. You can tell

by the noon shadows their fedoras cast, half-curtaining
etched faces, they've seen it all, done the Scrambler,

Tilt-A-Whirl, been spun, whipped in scarlet, yellow,
paid their quarters since they were boys, after planting

rows of Sugar and Gold to sell at roadside stands
to buy entrance to just this moment,

when the Round-Up cages start to rise,
and trailers pull in, unloading oxen, Holsteins,

Clydesdales, flinging dust, as stalls
of fried dough and sausages waft sweet grease

across fields. You can tell these men have sampled
elderberry jellies, judged lambs; they've played

the Mouse Game, Ring Toss, been lost
in the Glass House, watched fire-eaters,

the crush of old beaters at Demo Derby,
you can tell by the way they lean into their thighs,

they know the whole of it, the highs brought low,
weathered grass bent, the dust dispersing

into cotton candy blue, then upended,
landing on packed ground.

Winter Island

Come inside this pale gray day,
woodstove ribs breathing heat,
this blazing orange answer to north's

siphoned colors and coming cold,
drawing us close as lovers as the last
squawking *V* of geese embers south.

Praise this iron island making ashes
of heartwood, as no fire this day will make
of us: praise the scent of birch smoke

from fallen limbs, stove shouldering the pot
steaming with buttered onions, carrots,
soup bubbling orange as the fire

inside us, which gives itself to flame.
Let's huddle in with our differences,
warm our hands, hold out our bowls,

this temple we come to on the darkest
of days, this nave for harvest's sacrament,
deep appreciation for each felled tree

we break open in stove-lengths
from its trunk. Hear the music
of the metal creak and iron clunk,

as we stoke our blazing haven
this gray day, drop another log
onto bedded red coals.

He Dreamed of Flying

I imagine my father-in-law's fate,
RAF end, and not POW,

my husband, his firstborn,
not born. I imagine

mushroom death, red canna
rising from radiated earth, seared,

imagine Manhattan a fiction,
sorrows folded into paper cranes.

Guards refrain: *We'll never surrender—
first prisoners die.*

I think of Eleanor's daily column
making an aching nation feel secure:

To end the causes of war,
painting a peaceful landscape,

on a canvas of woven flax,
sown in blistered earth.

Ghost of chipping sparrow
plucking crisped stems,

summoning nectar
from mutated blue blossoms.

I imagine my husband's illness,
holding on for our daughter's vows,

and how infants were swaddled in linen
because it would outlast them.

Perfection

You are the faultless blonde
the teacher praises
for any answer,
the spotless kitchen
never cooked in,
ivory living room
and glass table
that never shatters,
vinyl-covered settee
never sat on.

You are slick
at pick-up sticks,
never knocking
the whole pile over.
You are chimera,
supernova searing
as you burn your insides out.
Your flawless diamond
facets promise to make
everything that isn't,
all right.

You, the centered bowl
of plastic fruit at the table
of shut-ins I visit,
shining golden pears,
red apples, purple grapes
I know aren't real,
but want to bite into anyway.

Time

The way I ease
into a moment,

like a mole
into its home,

unblinking
as a garter snake

baking snugly in sun,
unhurried, un-slow,

minding my own ticking.
Sand compressed

to stone, wind re-sculpting
dunes, re-ordering this

universe and the next,
burning out

and birthing stars,
never looking back

or forward, existing
in you, a lamp post

for the light
of eternity.

Fall Song

Vivaldi of falling leaves, violin strings,
symphony of all summer has come to—

last juices leaving limbs, drawing in,
leaf crackle of our vinyl 33 needle

note-pressed in grooves of your goodbye.
Birch leaves yellowing into brown curls

like your arms closing around me, maples
out-glowing their green, saying *notice*,

saying *whoop-tee-doo,* saying don't waste
this change, savor what will drop, grant cover

from frost, like sheets we slept between.
The beeches hold on as you did at the end—

your showy splendor measured in shadow,
your flare too much to last, like sunflowers

painted by your namesake. Nothing plain in you,
not one cell gave way without sparks from the bow.

How much you passed on to our children,
tender as leaf veins, coloring the world after you.

I stand listening to the blinding of leaves,
their commanding shiver.

Sweet Elegy

Oh, glass jars of fireballs and gumballs,
root beer barrels, cinnamon swirls,
caramels and taffy, the wonderment,
a grocer's shelf discovered for a cent.

Visits, each had its own sweet
greeting: the woman who raised goats
bent over the stove wood-spooning
thickening brown-sugared cream into penuche.

The milk lady gave lemon drops
when we bought quarts of fresh Jersey.
At home, hot fudge bubbled in a pot,
poured on dolloped vanilla

ice cream, maraschino cherry
on its throne. I still dream
of my hand in the black licorice,
being caught climbing to reach

the bowl over the kitchen cabinet—
the elder child trusted to fudge-coat
peanut butter and coconut for guests.
Oh, newly unsuitable confections,

in my museum of sweetness,
you never lessen, though my system
rejects you. No more s'mores
or gold-wrapped Christmas quarters,

every form of chocolate I lament:
creamy milk, dark and white,
dissolving like love on the tongue,
I lay to rest my taste for you.

When you call, I cradle the phone,
but don't answer, savoring every memory,
each dream of finer things,
sweet longing without end.

Invitation

Come with me to Pemaquid's shore
   late afternoon when the sun's lids
     close red and moist
over the weeping ocean
   streaking gray sand
     leaking as if to harrow
beach peas and peat
   wild yarrow's ghostly blossoming
     and flax-colored grasses
       gone to seed.

Come with me to inlets
   where foam feathers
     into pools we waited
all our lives to enter,
   where winds brush the surface
     of what we never said
not dipping into what we wished
   or knew how to express,
     our children's best becoming
tide pools of unexpected treasure
   bright star fish
     and flowering purple urchin.

Come with me again
   to this teeming shore
      where we can leave all
we asked of each other
   steeped in these waters
      to a briny tea
we drink saying
   what we couldn't then
      where we can stay
tucked among rocks
   like a pair of herring gulls
      wading in the waves
that carried
   your ashes away . . .

Chiang Mai, City of Temples

Gold domes, gold painted entryways,
we cross shoeless over white stones

past novice monks in orange robes
exposing their beliefs, as did Siddharta,

as here the *maha-thera* teaches
untrained minds: *on knees bow*

*three times. Seated, let rise thought,
emotion, smoke burning off.*

Discomfort in my shoulders, back, hips,
Name it, he says, *paining, paining.*

I breathe through ache of stillness,
of striving to just be.

Become empty as your image in the mirror.
Scent of agarwood, waves of quiet,

a hundred reasons to get up, move
from before the closed eyes,

the silent gold statue of Buddha,
teacher, who had first to walk away

from suffering, to find freedom
seated in selflessness.

See you on the other side,
said the driver who dropped me off

the day I entered the temple.

After the Long Winter

First gush of brook,
first buds high on the maples
closest to sun,

first robins flock, peck,
bounce
under boughs,

surprised, but not daunted
by overnight snow cover,
pecking through it with grit,

Hello, blanket of light
melting lingering frost, uncovering
spruce trees, chickadees,

finches' slow green
to gold. Hello glossy
rivulets crossing roads,

fields, cabin-fevered eyes.
Dense, voluptuous air
clearing throats,

layers of cold,
last year's pale lilies
folded over,

as we who in winter
forget the song,
yet from their feet

tiny green shoots
peek through,
drenched, beaming.

As If One

I remember the day
the power went out, damp,
nerve-pinged, mustard and rust
leaves spiraling, driving west,
big-eyed, tawny, intent to find
a place where answers
landed like hooves on packed earth.
I was curious, went too close,
leaping in, trusting.

The fawn today samples the front lawn
from its hillside bed, nestling the garden,
the grass hollow where its lean torso,
sodden with hollyhocks and carrots,
ventures for crab apples, too close
to the road, not knowing trucks
slow during rutting season, hunters
loading for anything with antlers.

Will you grow *spike* horns by next fall?
I watch, not moving as to frighten you
into harm, like the day it happened
to me, pinned down on tall grass,
leaving a doe-shaped imprint
seen only if you look out for it.

III.

Well Being

Let us be known
for the plea, sea to sea—one country,
lakes, plains, city streets,
essential work rewarded
long past pandemic disease.
Fairness regardless of skin or origin,
inequity's truth an epiphany,
warding off war a gain.

Let us be known
for Lincoln and King,
for questioning, inventing,
justice boring through
smokescreens, through hate
berating those dragging their bones
as the richest gain riches.

Let us be known
for opposing those
who sharpen their claws
on our daughters' plea
for a new economy
steeped in well being.

Let us be known
for clearing the sky for better lives,
now and then—an extra slice of pie,
known for the falcons' wingbeat
freeing seas of hungry children
as the raptor's shadow passes,
dropping bills like uneaten seeds.

Aubade

after the mystics

can your mind
hold both
sun and night
shadows of starlight
flowering
like psalms
songs of songs
where fear
has no chamber
heart no shame

can you take in
both oriole air
and winter's river
this love
that your hands
need not hold

can you sleep
within its canopy
waking beside your dearest
to dawning knowledge
lighting your farthest
darkest reaches

that in the beginning
and since
the beginning
there is no end
to this love

Yoga of Poetry

Ears between our elbows
    tailbones to sky
sonnets flushing *Om*
    heart to palm,

spine's inverted triangle
    hamstring, thigh.
Downward dog pantouming

through the upside down of us,
    releasing stress,
lengthening our breath,
    and may I suggest

odes to back stretch
    Namaste to you.
Unstringing tendons of tension

through star-fished fingers,
    Achilles pressing into red earth
sweet oil of saxophone,
    spoon lick of light.

Couplets melting nerve endings,
    blazing airways
through a stricken country,

softening the tongue of us
    with heads
between our knees.

Marking Time

Wait, don't go,
the field's saffron
with cricketsong,
jewelweed more orange
than the strange
socks I bought you,
to match your new
favorite shoes.

Don't worry if no one
asks about your spaceship,
your orange ball that whips
and splits into magnets of legs,
or if they call you sensitive,
introspective, don't want to play
your transforming games
of time-traveling penguins.
For now, shiver, weep
beside me. I won't speak.
If you reach for me
I'll close around you until
we both stop trembling.

Our separation—
"Two hundred sixteen-
thousand minutes . . . thirteen million
one hundred fifty-thousand seconds.
When can I come again?"

For once I don't say, soon.
The sun's tangerine weight
empties behind the hill,
but still time to make
our magic macaroons, to take
on our next visit to the moon.

Lament

Deep beneath this human
    comeuppance of ninety degrees,
unheard of this far north,

hot air suffocating the day,
    insects inching like the Poles
to warming climes, heat dripping

from finch feathers, window
    casings, wild ginger leaves,
as Earth weeps.

Lightning un-bottled,
    fire-bombing dry brush
burning hubris away.

Even the Jurassic survivor
    sequoias' adaptive bark
can't withstand this crisis.

Bless the poor
    as they inherit
Earth's less amenable gasses

and lost habitat, the last
    Arctic fox making extra tracks
to confuse fruitless pursuit.

Sing bluebird, soar condor,
    prepare to scavenge
your last great feast.

We give notice,
    cry out:
blessed are those
who do not know
    what is to come.

Last Night the Supermoon

Forgive me for not noticing
the indigo February sky,

birches peeling their winter skin
revealing raw pink beneath.

I overlooked wild turkey's
blooming copper and metallic rose

as the males danced, barely noticed
their splay-toed tracks,

missed chickadees, didn't listen
to the winged glee.

But last night, the moon came
to my window like your soul,

and I could not look away.
Brimming through the curtain's gap,

your apricot glow lay full beside me.
I could not sleep or fall into dreams,

the whole outdoors a dance floor
calling me to polka into the light.

Mama waltzed there, sure-footed
in her mismatched dots and plaid,

her belly laugh, quoting Longfellow
like a pro, as she spun you, Vincent,

though you never danced in life—
but I smell the mango, curry, musk

of your hair in the cold-struck air.
You've come to show me you're light

on your feet, that your soil test
made it to space this night

you worked the moon,
and it worked on me.

Seed Exchange

Wintered-over, waiting to trade snow for spring rain,
wool mittens for a tin of amber maple,

we come down from the hills and small family farms,
driving pickups, Outbacks, rusted GMC's,

dreaming of green beans, beets, waves of sugar and gold,
kernels I would plant as Dad harrowed rows.

Smell of leaf mold, compost, hands in loam—at home
with shovel, hoe, picking stones surfaced by frost.

Took something to get you off the roost, says my egg lady,
her beige mask stenciled, *No GMO's.*

The preschool teacher with a canvas tote redolent of lanolin,
adds *Grandma Mary's Tomato* to the town hall display

of saved seeds: *Deer Tongue Lettuce,
Easter Egg Radish, Guernsey Parsnip,*

provenance of the fire chief's *White Scallop Squash,*
written in the lines of his Abenaki profile.

The road foreman chooses packets of *Oxheart Carrots*
for his wife's pot pie. *She'd a come, but her MS acted up.*

Always had good luck with your father's Soldier Beans.
I brought pumpkin seeds, enough to sow a field,

as Dad did after the war. Open-pollinated,
seeds return to the womb

to root with the beetle, the ant, the worm,
turning *Fairy Tale Pumpkins* into coaches,

unused roadside plots into "giving gardens."
A way to get through it, says the Town Clerk.

Little Marvel Peas unfolding overnight,
covenant of chrysalis and gossamer-wing—

a commotion of growers cold-struck as the moon
we plant by, for the sake of generations.

What Circled Us

to my skeptic husband

You say there are no halos,
no glorioles, no coronas at night
no headdress of tenderness,

no crown molding hope
for humble ceilings. You say
I only imagine true medicine rings,

these healings, buffalo blood beating
in chests pressed against Earth's skull,
ribs holding an unbroken heart.

Let autumn winds brush
milkweed's silk against your lips,
slipped from its hollowed womb,

let snow kiss your eyelids
as you stand alone,
fingering your ring,

remembering cooking's cumin
scent against my skin,
till beauty begins to ring true.

See the glow of have-nots
we fed under a Harvest Moon,
the nimbus of streetlights

and headlights, of bright strings
spiraling from eaves—
we had reason for optimism.

The Way You Pick

Blackberries drip
with afternoon sun,
burgundy eyes
deep with late season.

A price to reach,
thick-sleeved
in the tangled heat,
risk the black bear
that tromped
the outer brambles.

These fecund hours
where the ripest seeds
burst from jelly cases
like jewelweed
from fertile pods,
like the newborn
from a daughter's womb,

shocked by light,
lost but for the doctor's
deft hands, separating
cleaved placenta,
working fast,

the way you pick, by feel,
watching for the bear
returning through heat
to thorn and vine,
as you hold the infant's
moist cheek against yours,
swaddle vanilla-musk,

your daughter not yet aware
of what she almost lost;
that blackberry canes
make peace with beating sun
with thrash and trample,
gamble hunger
to seed again.

Just This

When a six-year-old
googolplexes my love note,

when bird calls are all that is close
I want only to name the birds by their song,

to glean the sound-rich sky,
bluebird's *tu-a-wee,*

warbler in its pine retreat,
to distinguish kingfisher's

rattle, nuthatch's *tooy, tooy.*
Dare to love

this googolplex, this air chorus,
whistling titmouse,

twittering finch. Separate
winged sounds by rhythm, pitch:

slow, sultry white-throated sparrow,
kinglet's, *see-see.*

I can only assuage the lump
of the world in my throat

with the hermit thrush's
liquid flute, mourning dove's

hoo-a, hoo, the rapid
anthem of wren, again, again.

What Lasts

We watched maples change
color, unlike us, leaves drop,
run races over the lawn

in the wind, much-needed
rain, darkening trunks
standing firm as dreams,

keeping me awake,
rooted so deep,
they will outlast me.

Be happy, you said,
head bowed, *Namaste.*
You did not shut doors,

fried sardine curry when
guests dropped in, dried
dandelion blossoms to steep

for tea, marigolds for steaming
baths. You outlasted Japanese
prison camps, cane beatings, hunger,

shaming guards, schoolchildren
shouting *Brown monkey*
through barbed fences.

You sought light slivers
burning through barrack walls,
grains of charred rice the cook

tossed out the window—
Receive them, you said. *It is life.*
Hold no hate. The quiet

of your soft gaze undermined
slights with a good word,
until you passed peacefully

as milkweed silk lofts
from the pod, bright
as the milky lantern

of stars that lasts the night.

Voice of the Tide

*A riptide swept away a family . . . in Panama City.
Beachgoers formed a human chain to rescue them.
—The Washington Post, July 11, 2017*

Know from the way I'm always changing,
the danger of complacency.

Easy to lull you with the rhythm of waves
lapping against rocks, piers,

your sure feet. I forge marshes, polish wood,
glass, cast plastics across sand,

across sculpted dreams—
but you can count on my rising

twice daily, drawn by the moon,
and withdrawing to expose

the otherwise hidden.
Brimming with life, I join lands,

even countries at war
with my blue-green expanse,

I froth and foam, colonize shores
with rockweed, air with brine,

in my steel depths, conceal mountains,
create clouds the wind sends where it will.

Know from the way I'm always changing
mournful waves play off deep unease,

each time I leave my mark
without malice, erase cliff-side castles

that won't feed you, as I can,
though I'm only drops, joined

like caring hands,
spanning wind-ripped currents

to save the drowning human family,
if they will assist me.

Letter to My Grandson Through the Wardrobe

The phoebe sings beneath the eaves,
robins you watched fledge last spring

return to just-hoed beet rows,
their chestnut and honey bodies

bobbing over turned dirt, wind sighing
on the hillside, lupine reseeding

in paths we lopped between
baffled hedges, hypnotizing scents

of bee balm, anise, grape hyacinth.
No, your Grandpa didn't pass

from the novel virus I shelter from
as I sand oak floors discovered

under four layers of linoleum,
barn red with white roses of polio,

then whispering green of measles,
a cracked beige layer with tiny vines

of diphtheria, and coughed up last,
a violet-blue whooping I hear in dreams,

floors we walked together in a house yellow as sun,
fenced by cedars which don't keep mortality at bay.

When can I visit? you ask. *My germs aren't bad.*
Your breath a couplet of hope, my ache a refrain

sung to the lion who can't come back to save us,
as I record a *Prince Caspian* chapter for you,

my kumquat, chestnut eyes,
lids lifted like the coats

inside the wardrobe
to this uncharted world.

Why I Called in Thinking of Rumi

I know you've grown tired
of endless days shut away;

it's not your nature,
even in a world gone dizzy.

I listen to your tremor,
my hands in dirt,

tossing rocks, bowing close
to feel roots throb,

companioning tomatoes
with cilantro and marigolds,

my feet bare, mud-clung,
palms filled, and I cannot

tell if they are just born
or old, resting a moment

on this cool mattress
where hollyhocks,

reseeded in pea rows,
burst into burgundy tears.

Beauty can do that—
outspend itself.

You can get lost
in pandemonium

or in time alone.
I'm saying I'm here,

half-swallowed,
by your hurt's

distant thrum
as we come through

this limbo, its shadow
off-loading in front of us.

I'll stay wrist-deep in humus,
pungent as Rumi chanting,

Darkness is your candle,
reminding you

of everything green
the earth can't help

but lift into the shining.

About the Author

Judith Janoo won the Soul-Making Keats Award, the Vermont Award for Continued Excellence in Writing, The Carol Vail Poetry Prize and the Anita McAndrews Poetry Prize for Human Rights. She was nominated for a Pushcart Prize and is a contributing editor of *The Mountain Troubadour.* Her poetry has appeared in journals including *Pedestal Magazine, Fish Anthology, The Pierian, Euphony, Sow's Ear Poetry Review,* and *The Bangalore Review.* Her chapbook, *After Effects,* was published by Finishing Line Press in 2019.

She collaborated with the harpist and pianist Linda Schneck to create a *Music and Word* presentation, "a journey from the despair of war to the hope of peace."

Born in a fishing village on the Maine Coast, Janoo lives in the Northeast Kingdom of Vermont on the land that feeds her, where she shares wood trails with black bear and white-tailed deer, and the smoke plume from her chimney goes straight up on cold days.

www.ingramcontent.com/pod-product-compliance
Lightning Source LLC
Chambersburg PA
CBHW030910170426
43193CB00009BA/801